OPEN YOUR GIFT

Compiled & Illustrated by

Trish Rudolph

WestBow Press books may be ordered through booksellers or by contacting:

WestBow Press
A Division of Thomas Nelson & Zondervan
1663 Liberty Drive
Bloomington, IN 47403
www.westbowpress.com
844-714-3454

All scripture quotations are taken from the New King James Version®. Copyright © 1982 by Thomas Nelson. Used by permission. All rights reserved.

ISBN: 978-1-6642-9946-7 (sc)
ISBN: 978-1-6642-9945-0 (e)

Library of Congress Control Number: 2023908536

Print information available on the last page.

WestBow Press rev. date: 05/16/2023

WestBow
PRESS®
A DIVISION OF THOMAS NELSON
& ZONDERVAN

Dedicated to my Mom,
Who brought me up in the Lord and His Word,

Preface

All you could hear was the wind howling and snow beating against the windows. Dinner was being kept warm in the oven. Tom, a thirty-two-year-old father of two, was late. At 8: 09, the doorbell rang. Tom's wife, Anne, opened the door. She collapsed when the police officer informed her there'd been an accident. In his rolled over car, Tom was found unconscious. The EMS couldn't revive him. Tom was gone. Gone forever.

Anne barely made it to their bedroom, sobbing not being able to breathe. However, shivering and cold, she reached for a sweater in the top of their closet. An unopened present under the sweater, fell to the floor. It said "To Tom, Love Dad." Why hadn't Tom ever opened it? Curious, Anne ripped open the box. Inside was_____. You fill in this blank.

What is the greatest gift you could ever receive? Take a minute right now, and make a list of the greatest gifts someone could give you. Really think about it. It can be anything and cost any amount of money. Write it down, fold it up, and keep it. You'll need it at the end of the book.

What if I told you that God has given YOU, the Greatest Gift Ever Given. And it's a free gift (Romans 5:15&18). It's just sitting there, waiting for you to open it. Have you opened it? Or is it unopened, and shoved to the back of your closet, like Tom's present? Don't leave God's Gift to you unopened. Tomorrow may be too late. Open it today!

CHAPTER ONE

What is the greatest gift you could ever receive? That question will be answered by the end of the book. But before we dive into this, we need to take a look at the integrity of the main source of this book, the Bible (God's Holy Word). You may ask how did we get the Bible. God tells us in 2 Peter 1: 20 & 21:

"knowing this first, that no prophecy of Scripture is of any private interpretation, for prophecy never came by the will of man, but holy men of God spoke as they were moved by the Holy Spirit." (NKJV).

Did these men of God write what they wanted? No, they were "moved by the Holy Spirit." God is the Author of the Bible, with holy men of God writing down what God told them to. That's why the bible is called God's Holy Word!

You may though still ask, how accurate is the Bible? God defends His Word, the Bible, in Hebrews 4:

"For the word of God is living and powerful, and sharper than any two-edged sword, piercing even to the division of soul and spirit, and of joints and marrow, and is a discerner of the thoughts and intents of the heart." (verse 12, NKJV).

Further, we read what God thinks about His Word, the Bible, in Psalm 138:

". . . For You have magnified Your word above all Your name." (verse 2, NKJV).

Wow! God Himself endorses the Bible!

If you still have doubt, here's one more verse about the Bible. In Titus 1: 1&2,

> *"Paul, a bondservant of God and an apostle of Jesus Christ, according to the faith of God's elect and the acknowledgment of the truth which accords with godliness, in hope of eternal life which God, who cannot lie, promised before time began,"* *(NKJV).*

Men may lie to you, but God cannot lie…His Word, the Bible, is truth. Another verse in Hebrews 6: 17 & 18 also states God cannot lie:

> *"Thus God, determining to show more abundantly to the heirs of promise the immutability of His counsel, confirmed it by an oath, that by two immutable things, in which it is impossible for God to lie, we might have strong consolation, who have fled for refuge to lay hold of the hope set before us."* *(NKJV)*

Now let's dive into God's Word, the Bible, and see what the LORD describes us as? He describes us as His sheep of His pasture in Psalms.

> *"For He is our God, And we are the people of His pasture, And the sheep of His hand."* *(Psalm 95:7, NKJV)*

> *"Know that the LORD, He is God; It is He who has made us and not we ourselves; We are His people and the sheep of His pasture."* *(Psalm 100:3, NKJV)*

The LORD is our Shepherd, who takes care of our every need (Psalm 23, NKJV).

The LORD describes further in Isaiah how He is our shepherd.

> *"He will feed His flock like a shepherd; He will gather the lambs with His arm, And carry them in His bosom, And gently lead those who are with young."(Isaiah 40:11, NKJV).*

However, in Habakkuk 1: 13, it says that the LORD is Holy:

> *"You are of purer eyes than to behold evil, And cannot look on wickedness..."(NKJV).*

God cannot look on wickedness because He is Holy. Are we Holy by nature? Can we ever be good enough so the LORD can look on us someday in heaven? No, because we ALL have sinned and we are NOT holy. In Romans 3 it states: ***"for all have sinned and fall short of the glory of God,"(verse 23, NKJV).*** And in Galatians 3:22: ***"But the Scripture has confined all under sin,..."(NKJV***).

Just think how easy it is to sin. Have you ever told a lie, even a small one...so someone didn't get hurt? Did you ever drive over the speed limit because you were late? Have you ever been mad at someone...about anything? What sins you ask? So you've lived the best life you could live....been good to your family...been good to your neighbors...but what about how God sees sin. Everyone knows the Ten Commandments (if not go to Exodus 20: 2-17 & Deut. 5:6-21). The Ten Commandments are also known as the law in the Bible. Jesus talked about not sinning in **Matthew 5:20-28, *"For I say to you, that unless your righteousness exceeds the righteousness of the scribes and Pharisees, you will by no means enter the kingdom of heaven. You have heard...'You shall not murder,...But I say to you that whoever is angry with his brother...shall be in danger of judgment...But whoever says 'You fool!' shall be in danger of hell fire...You have heard that it was said to those of old, 'You shall not commit adultery.' But I say to you that whoever looks at a woman to lust for her has already committed adultery with her in his heart." (NKJV).***

So AGAIN, can we ever be good enough so the LORD can look on us someday in heaven? No, because we ALL have sinned and are NOT holy. In Romans 3 it states: ***"for all have sinned and fall short of the glory of God,"(verse 23, NKJV).*** And in Galatians 3:22: ***"But the Scripture has confined all under sin,..."(NKJV***)

We all have sinned no matter how hard we try to be good. No one is perfect, and God knew this. This is why Jesus came to earth.

Chapter 2

This is why Jesus came to earth. In Philippians 2 it states:

"Let this mind be in you which was also in Christ Jesus, who, being in the form of God, did not consider it robbery to be equal with God, but made Himself of no reputation, taking the form of a bondservant, and coming in the likeness of men. And being found in appearance as a man, He humbled Himself and became obedient to the point of death, even the death of the cross" (verses 5-8, NKJV).

In addition, in John 1:14 we read the following:

"And the Word became flesh and dwelt among us, and we beheld His glory, the glory as of the only begotten of the Father, full of grace and truth."(NKJV).

Who was the Word? We go back in the chapter to read the Word was Jesus, God in the flesh. In John 1: 1-14 it says:

"In the beginning was the Word, and the Word was with God, and the Word was God. He was in the beginning with God. All things were made through Him, and without Him nothing was made that was made. In Him was life, and the life was the light of men. And the light shines in the darkness, and the darkness did not comprehend it. There was a man sent from God, whose name was John. This man came for a witness, to bear witness of the Light,

that all through him might believe. He was not that Light, but was sent to bear witness of that Light. That was the true Light which gives light to every man coming into the world. He was in the world, and the world was made through Him, and the world did not know Him. He came to His own, and His own did not receive Him. But as many as received Him, to them He gave the right to become children of God, to those who believe in His name: who were born, not of blood, nor of the will of the flesh, nor of the will of man, but of God. And the Word became flesh and dwelt among us, and we beheld His glory, the glory as of the only begotten of the Father, full of grace and truth."(NKJV)

Back in Matthew 1, Jesus's name is explained. We read:

"'And she will bring forth a Son, and you shall call His name JESUS, for He will save His people from their sins.' So all this was done that it might be fulfilled which was spoken by the Lord through the prophet, saying: 'Behold, the virgin shall be with child, and bear a Son, and they shall call His name Immanuel,' which is translated, 'God with us.'"(21-23, NKJV)

And in the Old Testament in Isaiah 9 it was prophesied of the coming of the Lord Jesus:

"For unto us a Child is born, Unto us a Son is given; And the government will be upon His shoulder. And His name will be called Wonderful, Counselor, Mighty God, Everlasting Father, Prince of Peace. Of the increase of His government and peace There will be no end, Upon the throne of David and over His kingdom, To order it and establish it with judgment and justice From that time forward, even forever. The zeal of the LORD of hosts will perform this." (6&7, NKJV).

And further we can read in Hebrews 2 the following:

> *"But we see Jesus, who was made a little lower than the angels, for the suffering of death crowned with glory and honor, that He, by the grace of God, might taste death for everyone. For it was fitting for Him, for whom are all things and by whom are all things, In bringing many sons to glory, to make the captain of their salvation perfect through sufferings Inasmuch then as the children have partaken of flesh and blood, He Himself likewise shared in the same, that through death He might destroy him who had the power of death, that is, the devil, and release those who through fear of death were all their lifetime subject to bondage… Therefore, in all things He had to be made like His brethren, that He might be A merciful and faithful High Priest in things pertaining to God, to make propitiation for the sins of the people"(verses 9 – 17, NKJV).*

The Lord Jesus came to earth to suffer and die for our sins…my sin…your sin.

Whatever sin it is, GREAT or SMALL, we needed Jesus to come and die on the cross for our sins.

> *Colossians 2:13- 15 "And you, being dead in your trespasses and the uncircumcision of your flesh. He has made alive together with Him, having forgiven you all trespasses, having wiped out the handwriting of requirements that was against us, which was contrary to us. And He has taken it out of the way, having nailed it to the cross"(NKJV).*

And with that Great Love He died for us …

Romans 5: 7-9 "For scarcely for a righteous man will one die; yet perhaps for a good man someone would even dare to die. But God demonstrates His own love toward us, in that while we were still sinners, Christ died for us. Much more then, having now been justified by His blood, we shall be saved from wrath through Him"(NKJV).

Jesus is talking in John 10:

"...Most assuredly, I say to you, I am the door of the sheep. All who ever came before Me are thieves and robbers, but the sheep did not hear them. I am the door. If anyone enters by Me, he will be saved, and will go in and out and find pasture. "I am the good shepherd. The good shepherd gives His life for the sheep...I am the good shepherd; and I know My sheep, and am known by My own. As the Father knows Me, even so I know the Father; and I lay down My life for the sheep"(verses 7-15, NKJV).

Isaiah 52 proclaims the death of Jesus. How bad was Jesus beaten during His crucifixion?

". . .So His visage was marred more than any man, And His form more than the sons of men;"(verse 14, NKJV).

He was so beaten, He was not even recognizable. In Isaiah 53 it further states:

"He is despised and rejected by men, A Man of sorrows and acquainted with grief. And we hid, as it were, our faces from Him; He was despised, and we did not esteem Him. Surely He has borne our griefs And carried our sorrows; Yet we esteemed Him stricken, Smitten by God and afflicted. But He was wounded for our transgressions, He was bruised for our iniquities; The chastisement for our peace was upon Him, And by His stripes we are healed. All we like sheep have gone astray; We have turned, every one, to his own way; And the LORD has laid on Him the iniquity of us all. He was oppressed and He was afflicted, Yet He opened not His mouth; He was led as a lamb to the slaughter, And as a sheep before its shearers is silent. So He opened not His mouth. For He was cut off from the land of the living; For the transgressions of My people He was stricken. And they made His

grave with the wicked-But with the rich at His death, Because He had done no violence, Nor was any deceit in His mouth. Yet it pleased the LORD to bruise Him; He has put Him to grief. When you make His soul an offering for sin, . . . By His knowledge My righteous Servant shall justify many, For He shall bear their iniquities. . . And He was numbered with the transgressors, And He bore the sin of many, And made intercession for the transgressors "(vs 3-12, NKJV).

Furthermore, in I Peter 2: 24, it states about the Lord Jesus:

"who Himself bore our sins in His own body on the tree, that we having died to sins, might live for righteousness- by whose stripes you were healed"(NKJV).

And one more verse...

"and from Jesus Christ, the faithful witness, the firstborn from the dead, and the ruler over the kings of the earth. To Him who loved us and washed us from our sins in His own blood."(Rev. 1: 5, NKJV).

CHAPTER 3

But Jesus dying on the cross for our sins is just half of what happened. Jesus, who had been dead for 3 days and 3 nights, AROSE. He got up from the dead.

He breathed again! His heart beat again and his lungs filled with air! He was Alive again!

You can read all the accounts in detail of Jesus' resurrection from the dead in the Gospels(Matthew 28, Mark 16, Luke 24, & John 20 &21). (Please note **in this book**, the appearances of Jesus after His resurrection are **NOT** in chronological order, but grouped under similar circumstances; and Mark 16 will NOT be covered).

In John 20, it states:

"Now on the first day of the week Mary Magdalene went to the tomb early, while it was still dark, and saw that the stone had been taken away from the tomb. Then she ran and came to Simon Peter, and to the other disciple, whom Jesus loved, and said to them, "They have taken away the Lord out of the tomb, and we do not know where they have laid Him."

Peter therefore went out, and the other disciple, and were going to the tomb. So they both ran together and the other disciple out ran Peter and came to the tomb first. And he, stooping down and looking in, saw the linen cloths lying there; yet he did not go in.

Then Simon Peter came, following him, and went into the tomb; and he saw linen cloths lying there, and the handkerchief that had been around His head, not lying with the linen cloths, but folded together in a place by itself.

Then the other disciple, who came to the tomb first, went in also and he saw and believed. For as yet they did not know the Scripture, that He must rise again from the dead."(verses 1-9, NKJV).

Also, in Luke 24 (verses 1-12), you can read this account:

"Now on the first day of the week, very early in the morning, they (the women of verses 55 &56 Luke 23), and certain other women with them, came to the tomb bringing the spices which they had prepared. But they found the stone rolled away from the tomb. Then they went in and did not find the body of the Lord Jesus. And it happened, as they were greatly perplexed about this, that behold, two men stood by them in shining garments. Then, as they were afraid and bowed their faces to the earth, they said to them, "Why do you seek the living among the dead? He is not here, but is risen! Remember how He spoke to you when He was still in Galilee, "saying, 'The Son of Man must be delivered into the hands of sinful men, and be crucified, and the third day rise again.'" And they remembered His words. Then they returned from the tomb and told all these things to the eleven and to all the rest. It was Mary Magdalene, Joanna, Mary the mother of James, and the other women with them, who told these things to the apostles. And their words seemed to them like idle tales, and they did not believe them. But Peter arose and ran to the tomb; and stooping down, he saw the linen cloths lying by themselves; and he departed, marveling to himself at what had happened."(NKJV).

In Matthew 28 (verses 1-20), we can also read of what the women encountered at the tomb, Sunday morning (3rd day after Jesus's crucifixion):

"Now after the Sabbath, as the first day of the week began to dawn, Mary Magdalene and the other Mary came to see the tomb. And behold, there was a great earthquake; for an angel of the Lord descended from heaven, and came and rolled back the stone from the door, and sat on it. His countenance was like lightning, and his clothing as white as snow. And the guards shook for fear of him, and became like dead men. But the angel answered and said to the women, "Do not be afraid, for I know that you seek Jesus who was crucified.

He is not here; for He is risen as He said. Come see the place where the Lord lay. And go quickly and tell His disciples that He is risen from the dead, and indeed He is going before you into Galilee; there you will see Him. Behold, I have told you." So they went out quickly from the tomb with fear and great joy, and ran to bring His disciples word. And as they went to tell His disciples, behold, Jesus met them, saying, "Rejoice!" So they came and held Him by the feet and worshiped Him. Then Jesus said to them, " Do not be afraid. Go and tell My brethren to go to Galilee, and there they will see Me." (NKJV)

In John 20 verses 11- 17 we read:

But Mary stood outside by the tomb weeping, and as she wept she stooped down and looked into the tomb. And she saw two angels in white sitting, one at the head and the other at the feet, where the body of Jesus had lain. Then they said to her, "Woman why are you weeping?" She said to them, "Because they have taken away my Lord, and I do not know where they have laid Him." Now when she had said this, she turned around and saw

Jesus standing there, and did not know that it was Jesus. Jesus said to her, "Woman, why are you weeping? Whom are you seeking?" She, supposing Him to be the gardener, said to Him, "Sir, if You have carried Him away, tell me where You have laid Him, and I will take Him away." Jesus said to her, "Mary!" She turned and said to Him, "Rabboni!" (which is to say, Teacher). Jesus said to her, "Do not cling to Me, for I have not yet ascended to My Father; but go to My brethren and say to them, 'I am ascending to My Father and your Father, and to My God and Your God.'"(NKJV).

Another appearance of Jesus after His resurrection is found in Luke 24 (verses 13-35):

Now behold, two of them were traveling that same day to a village called Emmaus, which was seven miles from Jerusalem. And they talked together of all these things which had happened. So it was, while they conversed and reasoned, that Jesus Himself drew near and went with them. But their eyes were restrained, so that they did not know Him. And He said to them, "What kind of conversation is this that you have with one another as you walk and are sad?" Then the one whose name was Cleopas answered and said to Him, "Are You the only stranger in Jerusalem, and have You not known the things which happened there in these days?" And He said to them, "What things?" So they said to Him, "The things concerning Jesus of Nazareth, who was a Prophet mighty in deed and word before God and all the people, and how the chief priests and our rulers delivered Him to be condemned to death, and crucified Him. But we were hoping that it was He who was going to redeem Israel. Indeed, besides all this, today is the third day since these things happened. Yes, and certain women of our company, who arrived at the tomb early, astonished us. When they did not find His body, they came saying that they had also seen a vision of angels who said

He was alive. And certain of those who were with us went to the tomb and found it just as the women had said; but Him they did not see." Then He said to them, "O foolish ones, and slow of heart to believe in all that the prophets have spoken! Ought not the Christ to have suffered these things and to enter into His glory?" And beginning at Moses and all the Prophets, He expounded to them in all the Scriptures the things concerning Himself. Then they drew near to the village where they were going, and He indicated that He would have gone farther. But they constrained Him, saying, "Abide with us, for it is toward evening, and the day is far spent." And He went in to stay with them. Now it came to pass, as He sat at the table with them, that He took bread, blessed and broke it, and gave it to them. Then their eyes were opened and they knew Him; and He vanished from their sight. And they said to one another, "Did not our heart burn within us while He talked with us on the road, and while He opened the Scriptures to us?" So they rose up that very hour and returned to Jerusalem, and found the eleven and those who were with them gathered together, saying, "The Lord is risen indeed, and has appeared to Simon!" And they told about the things that had happened on the road, and how He was known to them in the breaking of bread."(NKJV).

Still reading in Luke 24 (verses 36-48) :

"Now as they said these things, Jesus Himself stood in the midst of them, and said to them, "Peace to you." But they were terrified and frightened, and supposed they had seen a spirit. And He said to them, "Why are you troubled? And why do doubts arise in your hearts? Behold My hands and My feet, that it is I Myself. Handle Me and see, for a spirit does not have flesh and bones as you see I have."

When He had said this, He showed them His hands and His feet. But while they still did not believe for joy, and marveled, He said to them, "Have you any food here?" So they gave Him a piece of a broiled fish and some honeycomb. And He took it and ate in their presence. Then He said to them, "These are the words which I spoke to you while I was still with you, that all things must be fulfilled which were written in the Law of Moses and the Prophets and the Psalms concerning Me." And He opened their understanding, that they might comprehend the Scriptures. Then He said to them, "Thus it is written, and thus it was necessary for the Christ to suffer and to rise from the dead the third day, "and that repentance and remission of sins should be preached in His name to all nations, beginning at Jerusalem. And you are witnesses of these things."(NKJV).

Another place where Jesus shows Himself alive (after He arose from the dead) and eats with the disciples is in John 21.

In John 21 verses 1 – 14, we find:

"After these things Jesus showed Himself again to the disciples at the Sea of Tiberias, and in this way He showed Himself: Simon Peter, Thomas called the Twin, Nathanael of Cana in Galilee, the sons of Zebedee, and the two others of His disciples were together. Simon Peter said to them, "I am going fishing." They said to him "We are going with you also." They went out and immediately got into the boat, and that night they caught nothing. But when the morning had now come, Jesus stood on the shore; yet the disciples did not know that it was Jesus. Then Jesus said to them, "Children, have you any food?" They answered Him, "No." And He said to them, "Cast the net on the right side of the boat, and you will find some." So they cast, and now they were not able to draw it in because of the multitude of fish. Therefore

that disciple whom Jesus loved said to Peter, "It is the Lord!" Now when Simon Peter heard that it was the Lord, he put on his outer garment(for he had removed it), and plunged into the sea. But the other disciples came in the little boat...dragging the net with fish.

Then, as soon as they had come to land, they saw a fire of coals there, and fish laid on it, and bread. Jesus said to them, "Bring some of the fish which you have just caught." Simon Peter went up and dragged the net to land, full of large fish, one hundred and fifty-three, and although there were so many, the net was not broken. Jesus said to them, "Come and eat breakfast." Yet none of the disciples dared ask Him, "Who are You?- knowing that it was the Lord. Jesus then came and took the bread and gave it to them, and likewise the fish. This is now the third time Jesus showed Himself to the disciples after He was raised from the dead."(NKJV).

Jesus appeared to the disciples when they were behind closed doors. He showed them His hands and His side(John 20: 19-23). However, Thomas, one of the disciples, was not with them when they saw Jesus alive again(verse 24).

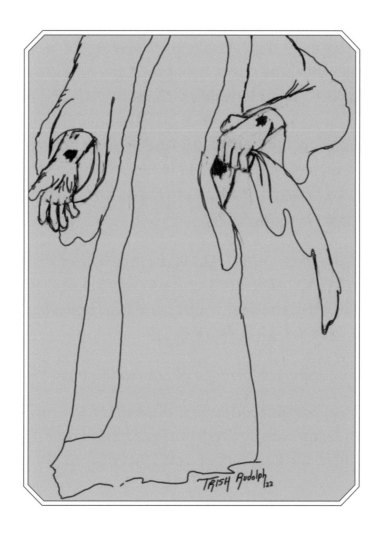

In John 20, it states:

"The other disciples therefore said to him, "We have seen the Lord." So he said to them, "Unless I see in His hands the print of the nails, and put my finger into the print of the nails, and put my hand into His side, I will not believe." And after eight days His disciples were again inside, and Thomas with them. Jesus came, the doors being shut, and stood in the midst, and said, "Peace to you!" Then He said to Thomas, "Reach your finger here, and look at My hands; and reach your hand here, and put it into My side. Do not be unbelieving, but believing." And Thomas answered and said to Him, "My Lord and my God!" Jesus said to him, "Thomas, because you have seen Me, you have believed. Blessed are those who have not seen and yet have believed."(verses 25-29, NKJV).

"And truly Jesus did many other signs in the presence of His disciples, which are not written in this book; but these are written that you may believe that Jesus is the Christ, the Son of God, and that believing you may have life in His name." (verses 30-31, NKJV).

After Jesus' resurrection, Jesus was seen by people for 40 days:

"to whom He also presented Himself alive after His suffering by many infallible proofs, being seen by them during forty days and speaking of the things pertaining to the kingdom of God" (Acts 1:3, NKJV).

How many people saw Jesus risen from the dead? How many witnesses saw that Jesus got up from the dead after 3 days and 3 nights? In I Corinthians it states He was seen by over 500 people at once, besides other times by the small groups of His disciples:

"For I delivered to you first of all that which I also received: that Christ died for our sins according to the Scriptures, and that He was buried and that He rose again the third day according to the Scriptures, and that He was seen by Cephas, then by the twelve. After that He was seen by over five hundred brethren at once, of whom the greater part remain to the present, but some have fallen asleep. After that He was seen by James, then by all the apostles. Then last of all He was seen by me also, as by one born out of due time" (15: 3-8, NKJV).

Who was seen by Jesus last of all? God was the author of I Corinthians through whose writing…Paul the apostle (I Corinthians 1: 1 &2). So who was the resurrected Lord Jesus seen by last of all? Paul the apostle…the one person who you would never think would ever, ever, ever believe was Saul (later Paul the apostle). Saul was at the stoning death of the apostle Stephen (Acts 7: 58), and was part of the Sanhedrin council because in *Acts 8:1, "Saul was consenting to his death* (the death of Stephen).*"* *In Acts 22:3-4,* Saul talks about his past, *"I am indeed a Jew, born in Tarsus of Cilicia, but brought up in this city at the feet of Gamaliel, taught according to the strictness of our fathers' law, and was zealous toward God as you all are today. I persecuted this Way* (the apostles movement) *to the death, binding and delivering into prisons both men and women,. . ."(NKJV)* Who was the one to get Saul to believe in Jesus? Which believer or apostle talked to Saul to get him to believe? It was Jesus, Himself… *Acts 9: 3-9. "As he journeyed he came near Damascus, and suddenly a light shone around him from heaven. Then he fell to the ground, and heard a voice saying to him, "Saul, Saul, why are you persecuting Me?" And he said, "Who are You, Lord?" Then the Lord said, "I am Jesus, whom you are persecuting."(NKJV)*

This story is amazing and can be read in detail in Acts 9. Further in the chapter 9, verse 17 we can read, *"And Ananias went his way and entered the house; and laying his hands on him he said, Brother Saul, the Lord Jesus, who appeared to you on the road as you came,...”(NKJV).*

But are you still doubting…even after Saul, who was having believers or Christians put to death, believed in the Risen Lord Jesus? If so, let's go on to read about when the apostles were taken to the high priests and council of the Pharisees:

> *Acts 5:33-39 “When they heard this, they were furious and plotted to kill them. Then one in the council stood up, a Pharisee named Gamaliel, a teacher of the law held in respect by all the people, and commanded them to put the apostles outside for a little while. And he said to them: . . . ‘And now I say to you, keep away from these men and let them alone; for if this plan or this work is of men, it will come to nothing; but if it is of God, you cannot overthrow it-lest you even be found to fight against God’” (NKJV).*

Did the gospel, the apostle's movement (of the death, burial, and resurrection of Jesus) die out with the apostles' deaths or is it not still here today? Is it of men or is it of God? A question everyone must answer.

What did Jesus do after He was seen by so many witnesses that He was alive?

In Acts Chapter 1 we read:

> *“Now when He had spoken these things, while they watched, He was taken up, and a cloud received Him out of their sight. And while they looked steadfastly toward heaven as He went up, behold, two men stood by them in white apparel, who also said, “Men of Galilee, why do you stand gazing up into heaven? This same Jesus, who was taken up from you into heaven, will so come in like manner as you saw Him go into heaven”(9-11, NKJV).*

Yes, Jesus is alive today and is coming back, but that's another study. Let's see where Jesus ascended to. Three different passages describe where Jesus ascended to and where He is right now:

> *"...It is Christ, who died, and furthermore is also risen, who is even at the right hand of God, who also makes intercession for us"(Romans 8:34, NKJV).*

> *"... seek those things which are above, where Christ is, sitting at the right hand of God"(Colossians 3:1, NKJV).*

> *"...through the resurrection of Jesus Christ, who has gone into heaven and is at the right hand of God, angels and authorities and powers having been made subject to Him"(I Peter 3: 21-22, NKJV).*

Jesus is ALIVE today, right now as you are reading this book!

> *"For though He was crucified in weakness, yet He lives by the power of God..." (2 Corinthians 13: 4, NKJV).*

CHAPTER 4

Greatest Gift Ever Given!

So what do you think is the Greatest Gift Ever Given? Hold your thought. However, let's see what God says the greatest gift is.

"For the wages of sin is death, but the gift of God is eternal life in Christ Jesus our Lord"(Romans 6: 23,NKJV).

"Jesus said to her, 'I am the resurrection and the life. He who believes in Me, though he may die, he shall live'(John 11: 25,NKJV).

"For by grace you have been saved through faith, and that not of yourselves; it is the gift of God, not of works, lest anyone should boast" (Ephesians 2:8-9, NKJV).

Now did you keep the piece of paper that you wrote down (at the beginning of the book) about what things you thought would be the greatest gift ever?

How do they compare with God's gift to you, ETERNAL LIFE with the FORGIVENESS of ALL your SINS?

First, your gift from God is by Grace. *"For by grace you have been saved…"(Ephesians 2:8, NKJV).* In Ephesians 2: 4&5 we read*: "But God, who is rich in mercy, because of His great love with which He loved us, even when we were dead in trespasses, made us alive together with Christ (by grace you have been saved),"(NKJV).* And again in Ephesians 1: 7, *" In Him we have redemption through His blood, the forgiveness of sins, according to the riches of His grace" (NKJV).* And in Acts 15:11*, "But we believe that through the grace of the Lord Jesus Christ we shall be saved in the same manner as they."(NKJV).* What does Grace mean? It means God's unmerited favor, getting something you do not deserve. Salvation through Jesus Christ is a gift of grace…by Grace alone…in Christ alone.

But how do you get your gift from God? It is nothing that you can do…no good works can give you salvation and eternal life. If you could work for it, it would not be a gift!

Again in Romans 6: 23: *". . . but the gift of God is Eternal life in Christ Jesus our Lord." (NKJV).* And again in Ephesians 2:8 & 9, *"For by grace you have been saved through faith, and that not of yourselves; it is the gift of God, not of works, lest anyone should boast."(NKJV).* This verse says in black and white *"that not of yourselves…not of works… "(Ephesians 2: 8 & 9, NKJV).*

No amount of giving to the poor, helping the homeless, tithing, rescuing someone from drowning…the list could go on forever. But NO AMOUNT of good works will get you the Greatest Gift Ever Given! So how do you get this gift from God? Jesus Himself tells Nicodemus how one can get eternal life. In John 3, verses 1- 14 we read:

"There was a man of the Pharisees named Nicodemus, a ruler of the Jews.

This man came to Jesus by night and said to Him, "Rabbi, we know that You are a teacher come from God; for no one can do these signs that You do unless God is with him. Jesus answered and said to him, "Most assuredly,

I say to you, unless one is born again, he cannot enter the kingdom of God."

Nicodemus said to Him, "How can a man be born when he is old? Can he enter a second time into his mother's womb and be born?" Jesus answered,

"Most assuredly, I say to you, unless one is born of water and the Spirit, he cannot enter the kingdom of God. That which is born of the flesh is flesh, and that which is born of the Spirit is spirit. Do not marvel that I said to you, 'You must be born again.' The wind blows where it wishes, and you hear the sound of it, but cannot tell where it comes from and where it goes.

So is everyone who is born of the Spirit." Nicodemus answered and said to Him, "How can these things be?" Jesus answered and said to him, "Are you the teacher of Israel, and do not know these things? Most assuredly, I say to you, We speak what We know and testify what We have seen, and you do not receive Our witness. If I have told you earthly things and you do not believe, how will you believe if I tell you heavenly things? No one has ascended to heaven but He who came down from heaven, that is, the

Son of Man who is in heaven. And as Moses lifted up the serpent in the wilderness, even so must the Son of Man be lifted up,"(NKJV)

"Son of Man" is Jesus and "lifted up" is referring to Him being lifted up on the cross when He was crucified for our sins. We continue in John,

"that whoever believes in Him should not perish but have eternal life. For God so loved the world that He gave His only begotten Son, that whoever believes in Him should not perish but have everlasting life. For God did not send His Son into the world to condemn the world, but that the world through Him might be saved" (3: 15-17, NKJV).

This famous verse says *"For God so loved the world that He gave His only begotten Son, that whoever believes in Him should not perish but have everlasting life." (John 3:16, NKJV).*

According to this verse who won't perish but have eternal life? *"whoever believes in Him" (John 3: 16, NKJV).* Another verse says *"For by grace you have been saved through faith..." (Ephesians 2:8, NKJV).* Through what are you saved? Faith In John 11: 25 Jesus states, *"I am the resurrection and the life. He who believes in Me, though he may die, he shall live." (NKJV).* Who do we have to believe in?

Jesus. ONLY believing in what Jesus did for us on the cross...He took our sins upon Himself so we could be forgiven! He died in your place, instead of you, for your sins. Simply, so you would not have to die for your own sins. In Hebrews it says, *"then He said, 'Behold, I have come to do Your will, O God.'. . . By that will we have been sanctified through the offering of the body of Jesus Christ once for all. . . . But this Man, after He had offered one sacrifice for sins forever, sat down at the right hand of God."(9-12, NKJV).* And another verse in Revelation 1:5 says about the Lord Jesus: *"...To Him who loved us and washed*

us from our sins in His own blood"(NKJV). So first, you need to believe what Jesus did for you...He died on the cross for your sins so you could be forgiven.

Besides believing Jesus died on the cross for you, to forgive your sins, you need to believe Jesus arose from the dead after 3 days and 3 nights in the grave. His heart started to beat again and his lungs filled with air. Today, He's alive seated in heaven at the right hand of the Father. In Romans 10 we read:

> *"that if you confess with your mouth the Lord Jesus and believe in your heart that God has raised Him from the dead, you will be saved. For with the heart one believes unto righteousness, and with the mouth confession is made unto salvation."(9 -10, NKJV).*

Chapter 5

Are you ready to open this gift from God? Let's unwrap your gift!

The Lord Jesus is talking in Revelation 3:

> *"As many as I love, I rebuke and chasten. Therefore be zealous and repent Behold, I stand at the door and knock. If anyone hears My voice and opens the door, I will come in to him and dine with him, and he with Me"(19-20, NKJV).*

In Luke Chapter 11, we read the Lord Jesus talking:

> *"So I say to you, ask, and it will be given to you; seek, and you will find; knock, and it will be opened to you. For everyone who asks receives, and he who seeks finds, and to him who knocks it will be opened. If a son asks for bread from any father among you, will he give him a stone? Or if he asks for a fish, will he give him a serpent instead of a fish? Or if he asks for an egg, will he offer him a scorpion? If you then, being evil, know how to give good gifts to your children, how much more will your heavenly Father give the Holy Spirit to those who ask Him!"(9-13, NKJV).*

If you're ready to receive this gift from the LORD, you can pray a prayer something like this...

Lord Jesus,

I confess I have a lot of sins that need to be forgiven and I'm sorry. I believe in my heart that you died for my sins on the cross, AND You arose from the dead after 3 days and 3 nights in the grave and are ALIVE today. I want you to be my Lord and Savior from now on.

Amen

You just received the greatest gift ever given, HIS Gift!

"I am the good shepherd. The good shepherd gives His life for the sheep (John 10: 11, NKJV).

"For you were like sheep going astray, but have now returned to the Shepherd And Overseer of your souls"(I Peter 2:25, NKJV).

Afterword

"But when the fullness of the time had come, God sent forth His Son, born of a woman, born under the law, to redeem those who were under the law, that we might receive the adoption as sons. And because you are sons, God has sent forth the Spirit of His Son into our hearts, crying out, "Abba Father!"

Therefore you are no longer a slave but a son..."(Galatians 4: 4-7,NKJV).

And again in Ephesians 1: 4 & 5 we read: "just as He chose us in Him before the foundation of the world, that we should be holy and without blame before Him in love, having predestined us to adoption as sons by Jesus Christ to Himself, according to the good pleasure of His will."

You not only have the gift from God of eternal life and forgiveness of all your sins, but you have been adopted as sons and daughters of God! Wow!

You are now going to heaven and nothing can stop you. *In Ephesians 1: 13 &14: "In Him you also trusted, after you heard the word of truth, the gospel of your salvation; in whom also having believed, you were sealed with the Holy Spirit of promise,..."(NKJV)* The promise of eternal life ...*I John 2: 25 "And this is the promise that He has promised us-eternal life."(NKJV) Furthermore, in John 10 we read, Jesus talking: "My sheep hear My voice, and I know them, and they follow Me. And I give them eternal life, and they shall never perish; neither shall anyone snatch them out of My hand. My Father, who has given them to Me, is greater than all; and no one is able to snatch them out of My Father's hand."(27-29, NKJV).*

Look what we have to look forward to: Read Revelations chapter 21 (only giving a few verses here). *Revelation 21: 1-7 "Now I saw a new heaven and a new earth, for the first heaven and the first earth had passed away. Also there was no more sea. Then I, John, saw the holy city, New Jerusalem, coming down out of heaven from God, prepared as a bride adorned for her husband. And I heard a loud voice from heaven saying, "Behold, the tabernacle of God is with men, and He will dwell with them, and they shall be His people. God Himself will be with them and be their God. And God will wipe away every tear from their eyes; there shall be no more death, nor sorrow, nor crying. There shall be no more pain, for the former things have passed away." Then He who sat on the throne said, "Behold, I make all things new. And He said to me, "Write for these things are true and faithful." And He said to me, "It is done! I am the Alpha and the Omega, the Beginning and the End. I will give of the fountain of the water of life freely to him who thirsts. He who overcomes, shall inherit all things, and I will be his God and he shall be My son."...(NKJV).*

That's our future! That's your future! The Greatest Gift ever given, HIS Gift, is now yours! You are a daughter or son of God! There is so much more for you to learn. The Bible verses in this book are only a very tiny glimpse of what the Lord has given you. Get the Bible and read it for yourself. Discover all that God has given you! Your journey has just begun.

Living Hope

". . .Who could imagine so great a mercy?

What heart could fathom such boundless grace?

The God of ages stepped down from glory

To wear my sin and bear my shame

The cross has spoken, I am forgiven

The King of kings calls me His own

Beautiful Savior, I'm Yours forever

Jesus Christ, my living hope"(Johnson & Wickham).

Works Cited

The Holy Bible. New King James Version, Thomas Nelson, 1982.

Johnson, Brian and Phil Wickham. "Living Hope." March 30, 2018.

Printed in the United States
by Baker & Taylor Publisher Services